SUPER SNAKES

ANACONDA

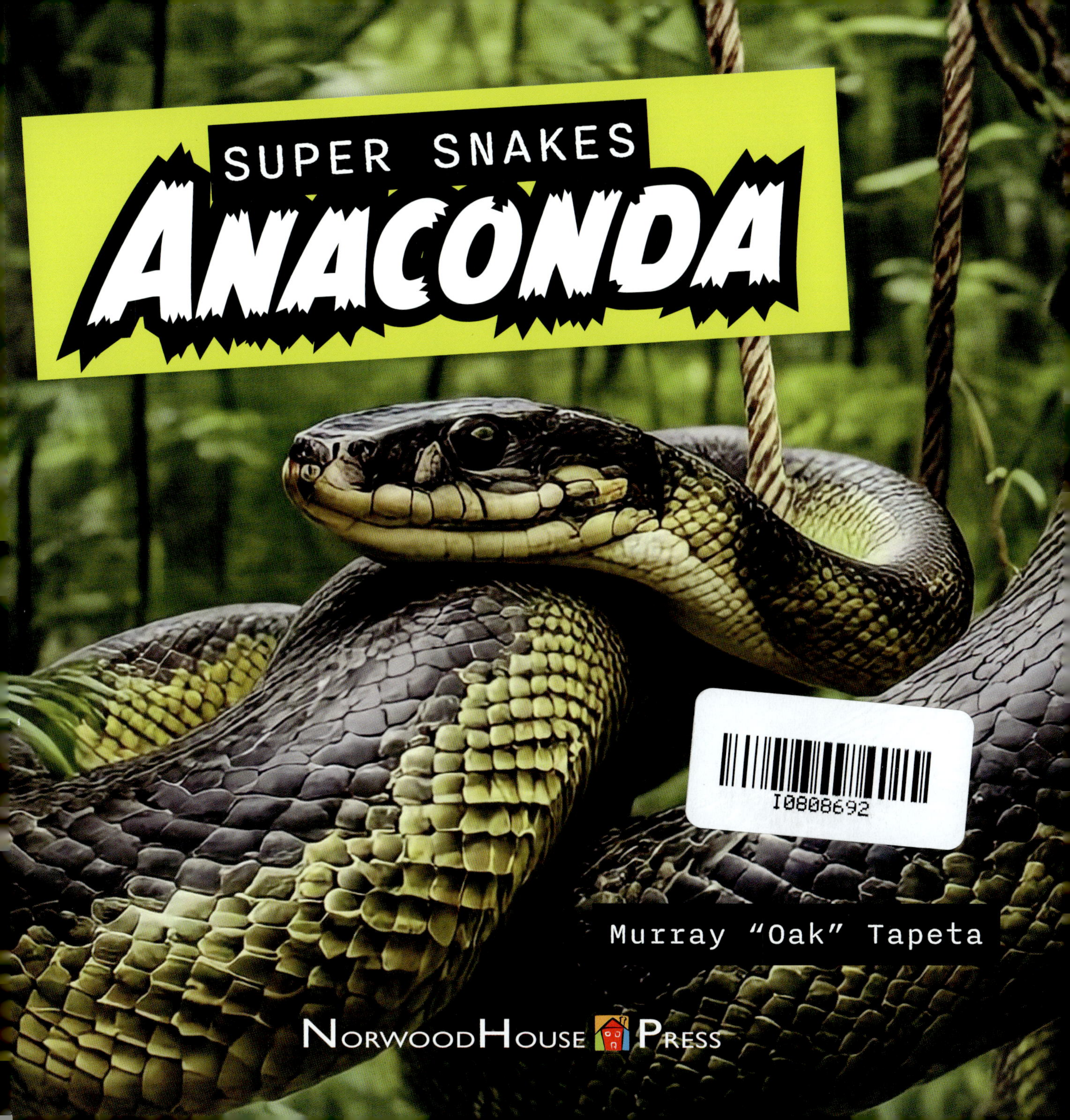

Murray "Oak" Tapeta

NorwoodHouse Press

I0808692

Cataloging-in-Publication Data

Names: Tapeta, Murray.
Title: Anaconda / Murray Tapeta.
Description: Buffalo, NY : Norwood House Press, 2026. | Series: Super snakes | Includes glossary and index.
Identifiers: ISBN 9781978575011 (pbk.) | ISBN 9781978575028 (library bound) | ISBN 9781978575035 (ebook)
Subjects: LCSH: Anaconda--Juvenile literature.
Classification: LCC QL666.O63 T374 2026 | DDC 597.96'7--dc23

Published in 2026 by
Norwood House Press
2544 Clinton Street
Buffalo, NY 14224

Copyright © 2026 Norwood House Press
Designer: Rhea Magaro
Editor: Kim Thompson

Photo credits: Cover, p. 1 mtayyab554/Shutterstock.com; p. 3 PeopleImages.comYuri A/Shutterstock.com; p. 5 RuqayaMai/Shutterstock.com; p. 6 Wirestock Creators/Shutterstock.com; p. 7 MuduPete/Shutterstock.com; pp. 8, 9 Vaclav Sebek/Shutterstock.com; p. 10 Vladimir Wrangel/Shutterstock.com; p. 11 guentermanaus/Shutterstock.com; p. 13 GUDKOV ANDREY/Shutterstock.com; p. 14 RMMPPhotography/Shutterstock.com; p. 15 chamleunejai/Shutterstock.com; p. 16 Ariawesomeness/Shutterstock.com; p. 19 Vadim Petrakov/Shutterstock.com; p. 20 slowmotiongli/Shutterstock.com; p. 21 AndiPu/Shutterstock.com;

All rights reserved. No part of this book may be reproduced in any form without permission in writing from the publisher, except by a reviewer.

Printed in the United States of America

Some of the images in this book illustrate individuals who are models. The depictions do not imply actual situations or events.

CPSIA compliance information: Batch #CSNHP26: For further information contact Norwood House Press at 1-800-237-9932.

Find us on

TABLE OF CONTENTS

What Is Special about Anacondas?

Anacondas are some of the largest and strongest snakes in the world. They are not poisonous. They have no **venom**. They use their massive bodies to squeeze prey animals to death.

What Do Anacondas Look Like?

There are four different anaconda **species**.

Anacondas can be green, brown, and yellow.

All anacondas have **markings**. The yellow anaconda has blotches, spots, and streaks of dark brown or black.

Anacondas are long and heavy. Females are larger than males. The green anaconda can weigh 550 pounds (250 kilograms). It can be 30 feet (nine meters) long. That is longer than three ping-pong tables!

Where Do Anacondas Live?

Anacondas live in South America. They like watery places. They are found near swamps, **marshes**, and rivers. Anacondas are fast swimmers. They can stay underwater for a long time.

Some anacondas climb trees. They wait on high branches. When a prey animal walks below, the anaconda drops and attacks.

How Do Anacondas Hunt?

Anacondas can wait weeks or months between meals. They eat fish, turtles, and other small animals. They also hunt large animals such as deer, wild pigs, and **capybaras**. Any animal that comes to the water's edge is in danger!

Anacondas hunt at night. Their senses help them find prey. Their **forked** tongues taste the air. Their large bodies feel **vibrations** on the ground and in the water.

Anacondas bite and grip with their **fangs**. They strangle prey animals by wrapping them so tight that they cannot breathe.

Anacondas swallow their prey whole. Their jaws have stretchy **ligaments**. They can open their mouths wide enough to swallow a human!

Anacondas do not fear other animals. Humans sometimes hunt the snakes for their skin. Some get captured to be sold as pets.

How Do Anacondas Reproduce?

A female anaconda does not lay eggs. A male **fertilizes** eggs inside her body. Six months later, the female gives birth to live babies.

As many as 100 anacondas can be born at one time! Baby anacondas are about two feet (under one meter) long.

GLOSSARY

capybaras (ka-pi-BAIR-uhz): large rodents without tails that live in South America

fangs (fangz): long, pointed teeth

fertilizes (FUR-tuh-lye-zis): provides the male parts that make a female's eggs able to grow into new life; joins male and female parts during mating

forked (forkd): divided into two branches or points

ligaments (LIG-uh-muhntz): tough bands that connect bones inside the body

markings (MAHRK-ingz): colored lines, shapes, or patterns on the surface of something

marshes (MAHR-shuhz): wetlands that form on low-lying ground near bodies of water

species (SPEE-seez): groups of similar living things that can reproduce with each other

venom (VEN-uhm): a toxic substance that is produced by an animal to harm or kill prey and enemies

vibrations (vye-BRAY-shuhnz): movements

Thinking Questions

1. On what continent do anacondas live?
2. What makes anacondas different from other snakes?
3. What do anacondas eat?
4. How do anacondas sense their prey?
5. How many baby anacondas can be born at once?

Index

About the Author

Murray "Oak" Tapeta was born in a cabin without plumbing in Montana. Growing up in the great outdoors, he became a lover of nature. He earned the nickname "Oak" after climbing to the top of an oak tree at the age of three. Oak loves to read and write. He has written many books about events in history and other subjects that fascinate him. He prefers spending time in the wilderness with his dog Birchy.